It's Electric!

Greg Roza

The Rosen Publishing Group's
READING ROOM
Collection™

New York

Published in 2003 by The Rosen Publishing Group, Inc.
29 East 21st Street, New York, NY 10010

Book Design: Ron A. Churley

Photo Credits: Credits: Cover, p. 1 © Ralph H. Wetmore II/Stone; cover (inset), pp. 1 (inset), 4 (upper left, bottom left, upper right, center right insets), 12 (top and bottom insets), 13 (all insets), 16 (bottom left inset), 18 (right inset), 19 (right inset), 21 (circuit breaker and outlet insets) © PhotoDisc; p. 4 (bottom right inset) © Tim Flach/Stone; pp. 7, 14, 15, 16 (battery diagram) by Ron A. Churley; p. 8 © Roger Ressmeyer/Corbis; p. 9 (left inset) © Mark E. Gibson/Corbis; p. 9 (right inset) © Paul A. Souders/Corbis; pp. 10–11 © C. Mooney/FPG International; p. 10 (inset) © Bettman/Corbis; p. 16 (Alessandro Volta) © Hulton/Archive; pp. 18 (left inset), 19 (left inset) © Bettman/Corbis; p. 21 (power station inset) © Peter Scholey/FPG International; p. 21 (electric substation inset) © Lester Lefkowitz/FPG International.

Library of Congress Cataloging-in-Publication Data

Roza, Greg.
    It's electric! / Greg Roza.
        p. cm. — (The Rosen Publishing Group's reading room collection)
Includes index.
    ISBN 0-8239-3708-9 (library binding)
    1. Electricity—Juvenile literature. [1. Electricity.] I. Title. II.
Series.
    QC527.2 .R695 2003
    537—dc21
                                    2001007996

Manufactured in the United States of America

For More Information
The Energy Planet
http://library.thinkquest.org/C004471/tep/en/index.html

Contents

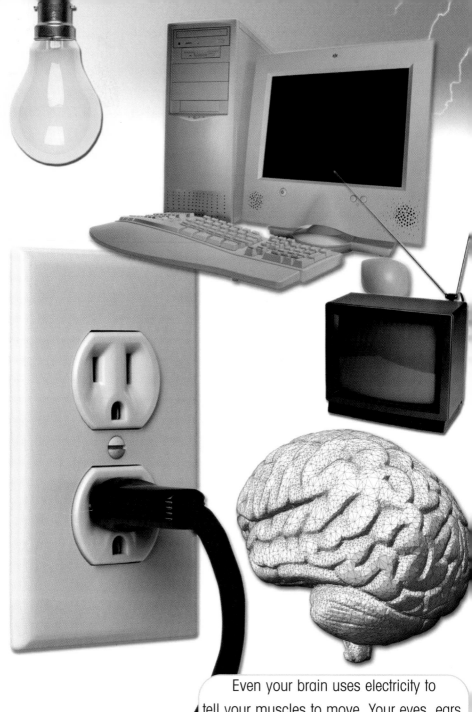

Even your brain uses electricity to tell your muscles to move. Your eyes, ears, and skin send electricity to your brain to tell it what you see, hear, and feel.

4

What Is Electricity?

What causes lightning to flash across the sky during a rainstorm? Why do you sometimes feel a shock after walking across a carpet and grabbing a doorknob? What makes your television, computer, refrigerator, and stereo work? The answer to all of these questions is electricity.

Electricity is a type of energy. Energy is a force that makes things work. We use electricity to do many things. Electricity lights our homes. It helps us search the Internet. It even helps us wash our clothes. Our world would be a very different place without electricity.

Electricity is possible because of tiny pieces of matter called **atoms**. Atoms are so small we cannot see them. Still, we know that they make up everything in the world, including people! To understand how electricity works, we need to understand more about atoms.

All atoms are made up of even smaller **particles** called protons (PRO-tahnz), electrons (ih-LEK-trahnz), and neutrons (NEW-trahnz). Protons have a positive **charge**. Electrons have a negative charge. Neutrons have no charge. Positive and negative charges attract, or move toward each other. Similar charges repel, or move away from each other. Atoms usually have equal positive and negative charges, so they are **neutral** (NEW-truhl).

Protons and neutrons form the center of an atom. Electrons circle the protons and neutrons very quickly. Electrons are small and light, and can sometimes be pulled away from an atom by other atoms. When electrons flow from one place to another, electricity is made. So electricity is the flow of electrons, or negatively charged particles.

An atom that has a positive or negative charge is called an ion.

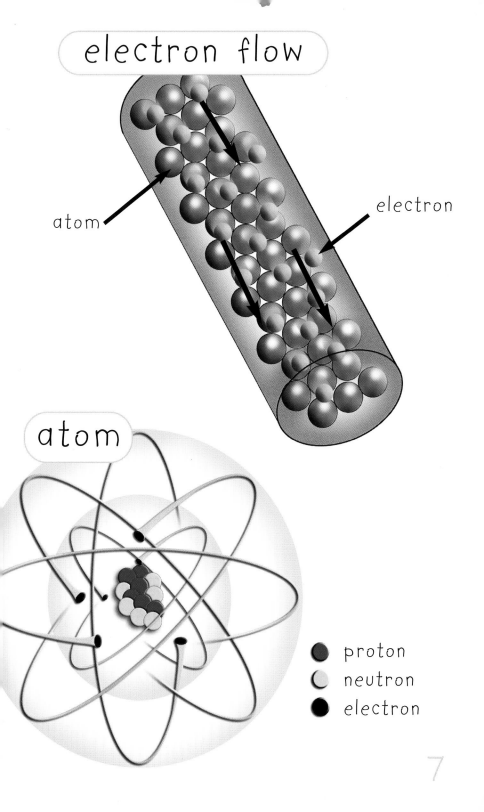

electron flow

atom

electron

atom

- ● proton
- ○ neutron
- ● electron

Static Electricity

When you walk on a rug, your feet rub against it and cause **friction**. The friction makes electrons move from the atoms in the rug to the atoms in your feet. These extra electrons give your body a negative charge. If you touch a doorknob, you will feel a shock. This is the sudden flow of electricity from your hand to the doorknob as your body gets rid of its negative charge. You will hear a snapping sound. If the room is dark, you might even see a tiny flash of light! This is static electricity.

Another way to see static electricity is to rub a balloon on your sweater. The friction makes electrons move from your sweater to the balloon.

This gives the balloon a negative charge and your sweater a positive charge. When you let go of the balloon, it will stick to your sweater. This is because the negative charge in the balloon is pulled toward the positive charge in your sweater.

You can do many kinds of experiments to see the effects of static electricity. You can visit your local science museum to see how it works. You can even use a balloon and your cat's fur!

Lightning is another example of static electricity. Inside a storm cloud, ice particles rub against each other as they are blown around by the wind. The friction causes a negative charge to build up in the lower part of the cloud. This negative charge causes a positive charge to form in the ground below the cloud. When the negative charge becomes strong enough, it is released as lightning and heads toward the ground.

Lightning usually hits objects that are [...] to the clouds, like trees and tall buildings [...] lightning hits buildings, it can cause a lo[t] damage. That is why some buildings hav[e] lightning rods on them. Lightning rods le[t] charges flow up to the clouds, lessening [...] negative charges. If lightning does strike, [...] hits the lightning rod. The lightning rod th[en] conducts the lightning harmlessly to the g[round.]

Benjamin Franklin discovered that lightning is electricity by doing a dangerous experiment. He tied a key to a kite string and flew the kite during a storm! The string picked up an electric charge from the lightning. The charge moved down the string to the key. Franklin had invented the first lightning rod!

Current Electricity

The type of electricity that we use to run our lights, computers, refrigerators, and everything else we plug into an **outlet** is called current electricity. Current electricity flows freely from one place to another as a stream of electrons.

Once current electricity is created, it is gone. So we need a way to control it and use it. We guide electricity where we need it by using wires. Remember how the lightning rod safely conducts lightning's electricity from the sky to the ground? Electrical wires also conduct electricity, so we call those wires conductors (kuhn-DUCK-tuhrz).

Some tools turn current electricity into other forms of energy. Lightbulbs turn electricity into light. Ovens turn electricity into heat. Fans turn electricity into motion, turning blades that move air around.

Most wires are made out of a metal called **copper**. Metals are very good conductors because their atoms have many free electrons. A free electron is an electron that can move from atom to atom.

Rubber and plastic are called **insulators** (IN-suh-lay-tuhrz). They do not conduct electricity well because their atoms have no free electrons. Insulators keep electricity from flowing where we do not want it to go. Electrical wires are wrapped in plastic so we can handle them safely.

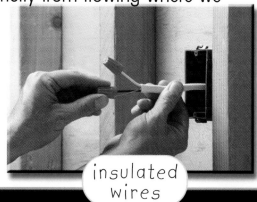

insulated wires

Current electricity is not possible unless it travels through a **circuit** (SIR-cut). A circuit is the path through which electrons flow. A circuit must form a complete circle in order for electricity to flow through it.

Electrons moving through a circuit are like cars and trucks moving over a drawbridge. When the drawbridge is up and the road has a gap in it, the flow of cars and trucks is interrupted. When the drawbridge is down, the cars and trucks can drive over it without stopping.

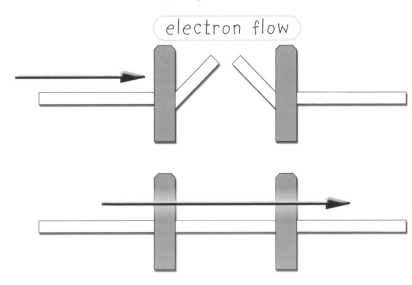

electron flow

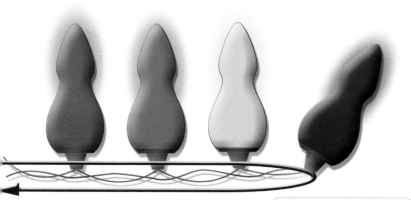

When you plug a string of lights into an outlet, the lights come on because you are completing a circuit. Electrons flow from the outlet, across a wire, and to the lightbulbs. Once the electricity reaches the last light, it comes back to the outlet across another wire. This completes or closes the circuit. If any of these parts are missing or broken, the circuit will be incomplete and the lights will not work.

Most things that use current electricity to work, like a television, have an on-and-off switch. When the switch is off, there is a gap in the circuit flowing from the outlet to the television. When it is on, the circuit is completed, allowing electricity to flow to the television.

Alessandro Volta

batteries

flashlight

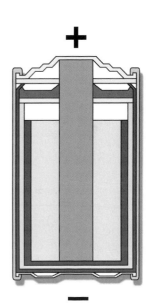

+

−

An Italian scientist named
Alessandro Volta invented the
first battery in 1800.

Making and Using Electricity

Where does the electricity that runs our lights, radios, televisions, and computers come from? The electricity that we use every day may come from **batteries** or **generators**.

Batteries contain **chemicals** that cause electrons to build up in one part of the battery. Protons build up in the other part of the battery. By connecting the two parts, a circuit is created. The battery pumps a steady electric current from the negative side of the battery to the positive side. When the circuit is broken, the battery stops making electricity.

In most flashlights, two batteries are placed end to end. When the switch is turned on, the circuit is completed. The chemicals pump electricity through the negative terminals, or ends, of the batteries, into the lightbulb, and then through a wire going back to the positive terminal of the first battery.

Generators are machines that turn movement into electricity. Generators need magnets to work. When a wire moves though a **magnetic field**, electricity is made.

Some generators have a magnet that spins near a coiled wire. Other generators have a loop of wire that spins between the poles of a magnet. Both kinds of generators create an electric current in the wire. This current flows through the wire as long as the movement continues. Some generators are powered by steam, water, wind, or human strength.

generator

A motor is the opposite of a generator. A motor turns electricity into movement. A wire that has electricity moving through it creates a magnetic field. When this wire is placed near a magnet, the two magnetic fields push on each other and movement is created.

electric motor

Electric motors are used to power many machines, such as toys, washing machines, and CD players. Some cars even run on electric motors!

Electricity in our homes comes from a power station. Power stations use water, steam, or wind to run very large generators. These generators produce a lot of electricity. Power cables take the electricity to **substations**, where the electricity's strength is changed depending on where it is going. Businesses and factories need stronger electricity than houses and farms.

Electricity enters your house through a fuse box or a circuit breaker. A fuse is a piece of wire that breaks if the current becomes too strong. This interrupts the circuit and keeps homes, people, and machines safe from electrical accidents. A circuit breaker uses magnets to do the same thing.

Electricity then travels through circuits to outlets throughout the house. Some machines have their own circuit because they need a lot of electricity to work.

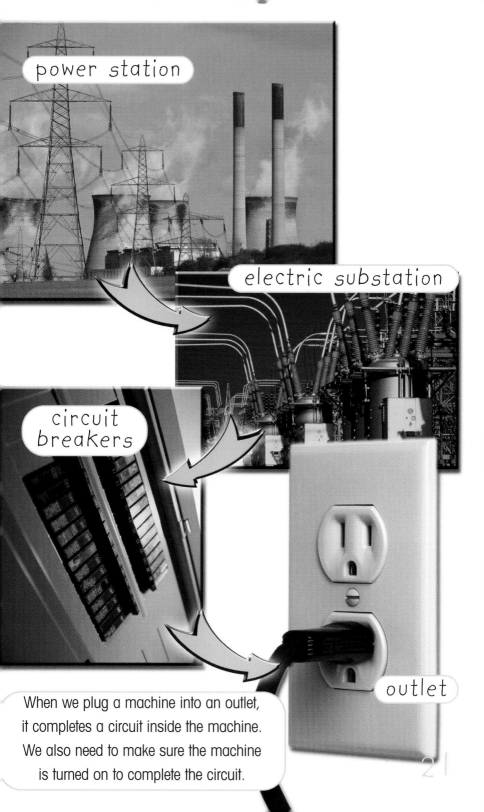

power station

electric substation

circuit breakers

outlet

When we plug a machine into an outlet, it completes a circuit inside the machine. We also need to make sure the machine is turned on to complete the circuit.

Staying Safe Around Electricity

     Electrical outlets can cause serious harm. The only thing you should ever stick into an outlet is a plug. Water is a good conductor, so stay away from outlets when your hands are wet or if you are standing in water. Tell an adult about outlets, plugs, and wires that look broken or burned. Put electrical wires where no one will step on them.

     Power cables outside carry a large amount of electricity and can be very dangerous. It is important to stay away from them. Stay far away from fallen power lines and anything they are touching. Don't climb trees that are near power lines, and never climb poles connected to power lines.

     If you are outside during a storm, stay away from tall objects like trees and things made of metal, like flagpoles. Go inside where it is safe and dry. Electricity is very helpful and very safe when we know how to act around it.

Glossary

atom   One of the tiny bits of matter that make up everything on Earth.

battery   An object that turns chemical energy into electrical energy.

charge   The amount of electricity in an object. A charge can be positive or negative.

chemical   Man-made matter that can be dangerous if not handled properly.

circuit   The path through which electricity flows.

copper   A soft, reddish-brown metal used in most electrical wire.

friction   The energy that comes from rubbing one thing against another.

generator   A machine that turns movement into electricity.

insulator   Something that does not conduct electricity, like plastic.

magnetic field   The space around a magnet or electric current in which a magnetic force occurs.

neutral   Something that is neither positive nor negative.

outlet   A place where we put an electrical plug.

particle   A very small piece of something.

substation   A power station between the generator and your home that changes the strength of the electricity.

Index